Bab' to love

M000227217

As soft as baby's skin, Bernat® Baby Blanket™ yarn is irresistible for crocheting all kinds of gifts for babies and toddlers. The super bulky weight lets you finish fast, and the durable plush polyester maintains its softness after repeated machine washing and drying. A range of fun baby shades is available for making wraps of all styles and sizes, as well as hats, scarves, ponchos, and more. There's so much to love!

About Spinrite:

Established in 1952, Spinrite LP is North America's largest craft yarn producer. It researches, develops, manufactures, and markets a variety of consumer craft yarn and pattern books for all segments of the market, from classic and cotton basics to novelty and fashion yarns. Its well-known brands include Patons, Bernat, Caron, and Lily Sugar 'n Cream. For more about Spinrite, visit Yarnspirations.com, a one-stop resource for everything that you need to create knit and crochet projects to suit any mood, budget, or occasion.

LEISURE ARTS, INC.
Maumelle, Arkansas

Ear Flap Hat

 **EASY**

SHOPPING LIST

Yarn (Super Bulky Weight)
Bernat® Baby Blanket™
[3.5 ounces, 86 yards
(100 grams, 78 meters) per skein]:
☐ #03233 Funny Prints - 1 skein

Crochet Hook
☐ Size L (8 mm) **or** size needed
for gauge

SIZE INFORMATION

Fits Head Circumference:
Small: 13¾" (35 cm)
Medium: 15½" (39.5 cm)
Large: 17¼" (44 cm)

Size Note: We have printed the instructions for the sizes in different colors to make it easier for you to find:
• Small in Orange
• Medium in Pink
• Large in Green
Instructions in Black apply to all sizes.

GAUGE INFORMATION

7 dc and 4 rnds = 4" (10 cm)
Gauge Swatch: 3¹/₄" (8.25 cm) diameter
Work same as Body through Rnd 2: 16{18-20} sc.

—— STITCH GUIDE ——

DOUBLE CROCHET 2 TOGETHER
(abbreviated dc2tog) (uses 2 dc)
★ YO, insert hook in **next** dc, YO and pull up a loop, YO and draw through 2 loops on hook; repeat from ★ once **more**, YO and draw through all 3 loops on hook (**counts as one dc**).

INSTRUCTIONS
BODY

Rnd 1 (Right side)**:** Ch 2, 8{9-10} sc in second ch from hook; join with slip st to first sc.

Note: Loop a short piece of yarn around any stitch to mark Rnd 1 as **right** side.

Rnd 2: Ch 1, 2 sc in same st as joining and in each sc around; join with slip st to first sc: 16{18-20} sc.

Rnd 3: Ch 1, 2 sc in same st as joining, sc in next sc, (2 sc in next sc, sc in next sc) around; join with slip st to first sc: 24{27-30} sc.

Rnds 4 thru 6{7-8}: Ch 3 (**counts as first dc**), dc in next st and in each st around; join with slip st to first dc.

FIRST EAR FLAP

Row 1: Ch 2, dc in next 6 dc, leave remaining 17{20-23} dc unworked.

Row 2: Ch 2, turn; skip first dc, dc2tog, dc in next dc, dc2tog, leave ch-2 unworked: 4 sts.

Row 3: Ch 1, turn; sc in first 3 dc, leave ch-2 unworked; finish off: 3 sc.

SECOND EAR FLAP

Row 1: With **right** side facing, skip next 8{9-10} dc on Body from First Ear Flap (front of Hat) and join yarn with slip st in next dc; ch 2, dc in next 6 dc, leave remaining 2{4-6} dc unworked (back of Hat).

Complete same as First Ear Flap; at end of Row 3, do **not** finish off.

EDGING

Ch 1, sc evenly around entire Hat; join with slip st to first sc, finish off.

BRAID

Cut 3, 40" (101.5 cm) lengths of yarn. Hold strands together and fold in half. With **wrong** side of one Ear Flap facing, insert hook in center sc on Row 3 and pull folded end of strands through st. Bring loose ends through loop and pull ends to tighten.

Braid ends until Braid measures approximately 6" (15 cm).

Secure end with a short piece of yarn; trim end of Braid.
Repeat Braid on remaining Ear Flap.

Design by Lisa Gentry.

Cowl

 **EASY**

Finished Size: 6½" wide x 20" circumference (16.5 cm x 51 cm)

Note: This Cowl is worked across the width,
allowing you to easily adjust the circumference.

SHOPPING LIST

Yarn (Super Bulky Weight)
Bernat® Baby Blanket™
[3.5 ounces, 86 yards
(100 grams, 78 meters) per skein**]:**
☐ #03305 Pink/Blue Ombre - 1 skein

Crochet Hook
☐ Size N/P (10 mm) **or** size needed
   for gauge

GAUGE INFORMATION

In pattern,
   (sc, ch 2) 3 times and 6 rows = 4"
   (10 cm)
Gauge Swatch: 6½"w x 4"h
   (16.5 cm x 10 cm)
Work same as Cowl for 6 rows.

INSTRUCTIONS

Ch 11.

Row 1 (Right side)**:** Working in
back ridge of chs *(Fig. 1, page 47)*,
sc in second ch from hook and in
next ch, ★ ch 2, skip next ch, sc in
next ch; repeat from ★ across: 6 sc
and 4 ch-2 sps.

Note: Loop a short piece of yarn
around any stitch to mark Row 1
as **right** side.

Row 2: Ch 1, turn; sc in first sc and
in next ch-2 sp, ch 2, ★ skip next
sc, sc in next ch-2 sp, ch 2; repeat
from ★ across to last 2 sc, skip
next sc, sc in last sc.

Repeat Row 2 for pattern until
Cowl measures approximately 20"
(51 cm) from beginning ch **or** to
desired circumference, ending by
working a **right** side row.

Joining: Hold the first and last
rows with **right** side together.
Working through **both** loops of
both layers *(Fig. 5a, page 48)*,
slip st in each st across; finish off.

Poncho

Shown on pages 11 & 12.

 **EASY**

SHOPPING LIST

Yarn (Super Bulky Weight)
Bernat® Baby Blanket™
[3.5 ounces, 86 yards
(100 grams, 78 meters) per skein]:
☐ #03616 Pitter Patter -
   1{2-3} skein(s)

Crochet Hook

☐ Size M/N (9 mm) **or** size needed
   for gauge

SIZE INFORMATION

Finished length from neck to straight edge:

Small: 4¹/₂" (11.5 cm)
Medium: 7¹/₂" (19 cm)
Large: 10¹/₂" (26.5 cm)

Size Note: We have printed the instructions for the sizes in different colors to make it easier for you to find:

• Small in Orange
• Medium in Pink
• Large in Green

Instructions in Black apply to all sizes.

GAUGE INFORMATION

In pattern,
   (ch 1, Cluster) 4 times and
   7 rows = 4" (10 cm)
Gauge Swatch: 6¹/₂"w x 4"h
   (16.5 cm x 10 cm)
Ch 13.
Work same as Body for 7 rows:
4 sc, 4 Clusters, and 4 ch-1 sps.
Finish off.

——STITCH GUIDE——

BEGINNING CLUSTER (uses 2 chs) (Insert hook in **next** ch, YO and pull up a loop) twice, YO and draw through all 3 loops on hook.

CLUSTER (uses next Cluster & sp) Insert hook in next Cluster, YO and pull up a loop, insert hook in next ch-1 sp, YO and pull up a loop, YO and draw through all 3 loops on hook.

INSTRUCTIONS
BODY

Ch 31{45-59}.

Row 1 (Wrong side)**:** Working in back ridge of chs *(Fig. 1, page 47)*, sc in second ch from hook and in next ch, (ch 1, work Beginning Cluster) across to last 2 chs, sc in last 2 chs: 4 sc, 13{20-27} Clusters, and 13{20-27} ch-1 sps.

Note: Loop a short piece of yarn around the **back** of any stitch on Row 1 to mark **right** side.

Row 2: Ch 1, turn; sc in first 2 sc, (ch 1, work Cluster) across to last 2 sc, sc in last 2 sc.

Repeat Row 2 for pattern until Body measures approximately 4½{7½-10½}"/11.5{19-26.5} cm from beginning ch.

SHOULDER

Row 1: Ch 1, turn; sc in first 2 sc, (ch 1, work Cluster) 2{5-8} times, sc in next Cluster and in next ch-1 sp, leave remaining sts unworked: 4 sc, 2{5-8} Clusters, and 2{5-8} ch-1 sps.

Continue working in pattern (Row 2 of Body) until Poncho measures approximately 11{15-19}"/28{38-48.5} cm from beginning ch.

Joining: With **right** side together and referring to the Diagram, slip st in each st across Shoulder working through **both** loops of **both** layers *(Fig. 5a, page 48)*; finish off.

DIAGRAM

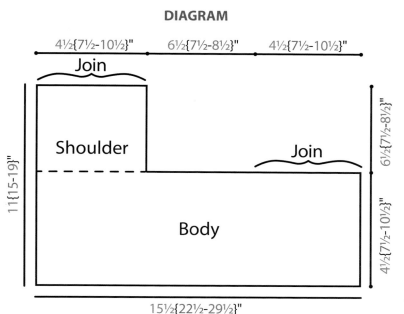

4½{7½-10½}"   6½{7½-8½}"   4½{7½-10½}"

Join

Shoulder   Join

11{15-19}"

Body

6½{7½-8½}"

4½{7½-10½}"

15½{22½-29½}"

13

Hooded Scarf

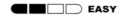 **EASY**

Finished Size of Scarf: 5" x 52¹/₂" (12.75 cm x 133.5 cm)

SHOPPING LIST

Yarn (Super Bulky Weight) **6 SUPER BULKY**
Bernat® Baby Blanket™
[3.5 ounces, 86 yards
(100 grams, 78 meters) per skein]:
☐ Color A, #03200 Baby Pink -
  2 skeins
☐ Color B, #03202 Baby Blue -
  1 skein

Crochet Hook
☐ Size M/N (9 mm) **or** size
  needed for gauge

GAUGE INFORMATION

In pattern,
   1 repeat (6 sts) = 3¹/₄" (8.25 cm);
   6 rows = 5" (12.75 cm)
Gauge Swatch: 7"w x 5"h
   (17.75 cm x 12.75 cm)
Ch 14 loosely.
Rows 1-5: Work same as Scarf.
Row 6: Ch 1, turn; working in both loops, sc in first st, 2 sc in next ch-2 sp, (sc in next st, 2 sc in next ch-2 sp) across; finish off.

STITCH GUIDE

2-DC CLUSTER (uses next 2 dc)
★ YO, insert hook in next dc, YO and pull up a loop, YO and draw through 2 loops on hook; repeat from ★ once more, YO and draw through all 3 loops on hook.
3-DC CLUSTER (uses next 3 sts)
★ YO, insert hook in next st, YO and pull up a loop, YO and draw through 2 loops on hook; repeat from ★ 2 times more, YO and draw through all 4 loops on hook.
5-DC CLUSTER (uses next 5 sts)
★ YO, insert hook in next st, YO and pull up a loop, YO and draw through 2 loops on hook; repeat from ★ 4 times more, YO and draw through all 6 loops on hook.

LONG CLUSTER (uses 5 dc)
★ † YO, insert hook in next dc, YO and pull up a loop, YO and draw through 2 loops on hook †; repeat from ★ once more, YO, working around previous 2 rows, insert hook in both loops of center dc of 5-dc group on Row 2 (Fig. A), YO and pull up a loop even with loop on hook, YO and draw through 2 loops on hook, repeat from † to † twice, YO and draw through all 6 loops on hook.

Fig. A

INSTRUCTIONS
BODY

With Color A, ch 98 loosely.
Row 1 (Right side): Working in back ridge of chs (Fig. 1, page 47), sc in second ch from hook and in each ch across: 97 sc.

Note: Loop a short piece of yarn around any stitch to mark Row 1 as **right** side.

To change colors, work last dc to within one step of completion (2 loops on hook), drop yarn; with new color, YO and draw through both loops on hook *(Fig. B)*.

Fig. B

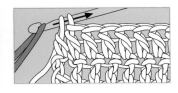

Row 2: Ch 3 **(counts as first dc)**, turn; 2 dc in first sc, skip next 2 sc, sc in next sc, ★ skip next 2 sc, 5 dc in next sc, skip next 2 sc, sc in next sc; repeat from ★ across to last 3 sc, skip next 2 sc, 2 dc in last sc, dc in same sc changing to Color B; do **not** cut Color A: 16 sc and 15 5-dc groups.

Row 3: Ch 1, turn; working in Back Loops Only *(Fig. 2, page 47)*, sc in first dc, ★ ch 2, work 5-dc Cluster, ch 2, sc in next dc; repeat from ★ across: 17 sc, 16 Clusters, and 32 ch-2 sps.

Row 4: Turn; working in both loops, slip st in first sc, skip next ch, 5 dc in next ch, ★ skip next Cluster and next ch-2 sp, slip st in next sc, skip next ch, 5 dc in next ch; repeat from ★ across to last ch-2 sp; cut Color B, skip last ch-2 sp, with Color A, slip st in last sc: 97 sts.

Row 5: Ch 2, turn; working in Back Loops Only, work 2-dc Cluster, ch 2, sc in next dc, ch 2, ★ work Long Cluster, ch 2, sc in next dc, ch 2; repeat from ★ across to last 2 dc, work 3-dc Cluster: 16 sc and 32 ch-2 sps.

Row 6 (Front trim)**:** Ch 1, turn; working in both loops, sc in first st, 2 sc in next ch-2 sp, (sc in next st, 2 sc in next ch-2 sp) 10 times, slip st in next sc, ★ skip next ch, 5 dc in next ch, skip next Cluster and next ch-2 sp, slip st in next sc; repeat from ★ 4 times **more**, (2 sc in next ch-2 sp, sc in next st) across; finish off.

HOOD

Row 1: With **right** side facing and working in free loops of beginning ch, skip first 32 chs and join Color A with slip st in next ch; sc in next ch, hdc in next ch, dc in next 27 chs, hdc in next ch, sc in next ch, slip st in next ch, leave remaining 32 chs unworked: 33 sts.

Row 2: Turn; slip st in first slip st, sc in next 3 sts, hdc in next 3 dc, dc in next 6 dc, work 2-dc Cluster, work 3-dc Cluster, work 2-dc Cluster, dc in next 6 dc, hdc in next 3 dc, sc in next 3 sts, slip st in last slip st: 29 sts.

Row 3: Turn; slip st in first slip st; sc in next 3 sc, hdc in next 3 hdc, dc in next 5 dc, work 2-dc Cluster, dc in next dc, work 2-dc Cluster, dc in next 5 dc, hdc in next 3 hdc, sc in next 3 sc, slip st in last slip st: 27 sts.

Joining: Fold the Hood in half with **right** side together; working through **outer** loops of **both** layers *(Fig. 5b, page 48)*, slip st in first 13 sts, leave last st unworked; finish off.

Design by Cathy Hardy.

Cocoon

 **EASY**

Finished Size: 23¹/₂" high x 28" circumference (59.5 cm x 71 cm)

SHOPPING LIST

Yarn (Super Bulky Weight)
Bernat® Baby Blanket™
[3.5 ounces, 86 yards
(100 grams, 78 meters) per skein]:
☐ #03615 Baby Yellow - 3 skeins

Crochet Hook
☐ Size N/P (10 mm) **or** size needed
   for gauge

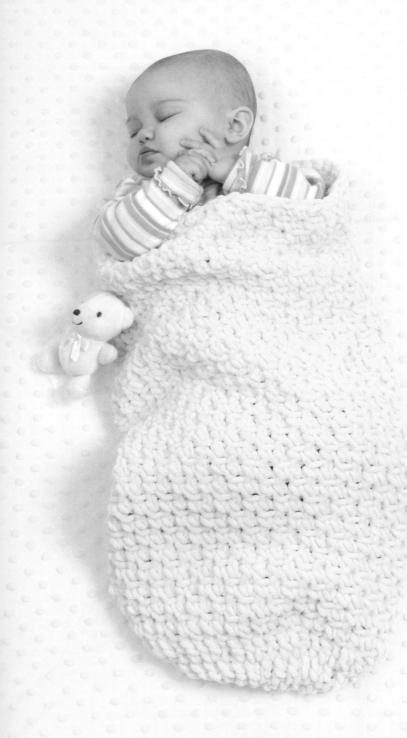

GAUGE INFORMATION

In pattern,
   7 sc and 6 rnds = 4" (10 cm)
Gauge Swatch: 5½" x 8"
   (14 cm x 20.25 cm)
Work same as Cocoon through
Rnd 2: 36 dc.

INSTRUCTIONS

Ch 9.

Rnd 1 (Right side)**:** Dc in fourth ch
from hook **(3 skipped chs count
as first dc)**, 2 dc in each of next
4 chs, 4 dc in last ch; working in
free loops of beginning ch *(Fig. 3,
page 47)*, 2 dc in each of next
5 chs; join with slip st to first dc:
24 dc.

Rnd 2: Ch 3 **(counts as first dc,
now and throughout)**, 2 dc in
next dc, (dc in next dc, 2 dc in next
dc) around; join with slip st to first
dc: 36 dc.

Rnd 3: Ch 3, dc in same st as
joining and in next dc, 2 dc in next
dc, (dc in next 2 dc, 2 dc in next
dc) around; do **not** join: 49 dc.

Because the repeat is an even
number of stitches worked
on an odd number of stitches,
a continuous spiral will form
automatically as you work. It is not
necessary to mark the beginning
of a round or to keep track of
which round you are on.

Pattern: ★ Sc in Back Loop Only
of next st *(Fig. 2, page 47)*, sc in
Front Loop Only of next st; repeat
from ★ around until Cocoon
measures approximately 23½"
(59.5 cm) from beginning ch;
slip st in next sc, finish off.

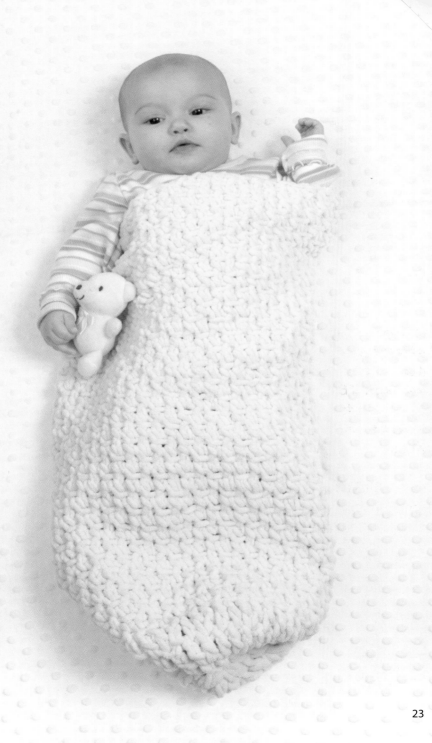

Girl's Car Seat Cover

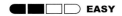 **EASY**

Finished Size: 15³/₄" x 22" (40 cm x 56 cm)

SHOPPING LIST

Yarn (Super Bulky Weight)
Bernat® Baby Blanket™
[3.5 ounces, 86 yards
(100 grams, 78 meters) per skein]:
☐ #03200 Baby Pink - 3 skeins

Crochet Hook
☐ Size N/P (10 mm) **or** size needed
   for gauge

GAUGE INFORMATION

In pattern,

    8 sts = 4$^1/_2$" (11.5 cm);

    4 rows = 4" (10 cm)

Gauge Swatch: 4$^1/_2$"w x 4"h

    (11.5 cm x 10 cm)

Ch 10 **loosely.**

Work same as Cover for 4 rows: 8 sts.

Finish off.

INSTRUCTIONS

Ch 30 **loosely.**

Row 1 (Right side)**:** Working in back ridge of chs *(Fig. 1, page 47)*, dc in fourth ch from hook **(3 skipped chs count as first dc)** and in each ch across: 28 dc.

Row 2: Ch 3 **(counts as first dc, now and throughout)**, turn; dc in next dc and in each dc across.

Row 3: Ch 1, turn; working in Back Loops Only *(Fig. 2, page 47)*, sc in first dc, dc in next dc, (sc in next dc, dc in next dc) across.

Row 4: Ch 1, turn; working in both loops, sc in first dc, dc in next sc, (sc in next dc, dc in next sc) across.

Row 5: Ch 3, turn; dc in Back Loop Only of next sc and in each st across.

Row 6: Ch 3, turn; dc in both loops of next dc and in each dc across.

Repeat Rows 3-6 for pattern until Cover measures approximately 22" (56 cm) from beginning ch, ending by working Row 6.

Finish off.

Boy's Car Seat Cover

Shown on page 29.

 **EASY**

Finished Size: 15³/₄" x 21¹/₂" (40 cm x 54.5 cm)

SHOPPING LIST

Yarn (Super Bulky Weight)
Bernat® Baby Blanket™
[3.5 ounces, 86 yards
(100 grams, 78 meters) per skein]:
☐ #03128 Little Cosmos - 2 skeins

Crochet Hook
☐ Size N/P (10 mm) **or** size needed
for gauge

GAUGE INFORMATION

In pattern,
  (Cluster, ch 1) 4 times = 4$\frac{1}{2}$"
  (11.5 cm);
  4 rows = 4" (10 cm)
Gauge Swatch: 5$\frac{1}{2}$"w x 4$\frac{1}{2}$"h
  (14 cm x 11.5 cm)
Ch 10.
Work same as Cover for 5 rows:
4 Clusters and 5 sps.
Finish off.

——STITCH GUIDE——

CLUSTER (uses one ch-1 sp)
★ YO, insert hook in ch-1 sp
indicated, YO and pull up a loop,
YO and draw through 2 loops on
hook; repeat from ★ once **more**,
YO and draw through all 3 loops
on hook.

INSTRUCTIONS

Ch 28.

Row 1 (Right side)**:** Working in
back ridge of chs *(Fig. 1, page 47)*,
sc in second ch from hook,
★ ch 1, skip next ch, sc in next ch;
repeat from ★ across: 14 sc and
13 ch-1 sps.

Row 2: Ch 1, turn; sc in first sc,
★ ch 1, skip next ch-1 sp, sc in
next sc; repeat from ★ across.

Row 3: Ch 4, turn; work Cluster in
first ch-1 sp, ch 1, ★ skip next sc,
work Cluster in next ch-1 sp, ch 1;
repeat from ★ across to last sc, dc
in last sc: 13 Clusters and 14 sps.

Row 4: Ch 1, turn; sc in first dc,
ch 1, ★ skip next Cluster, sc in next
ch-1 sp, ch 1; repeat from ★ across
to last Cluster, skip last Cluster and
next ch, sc in next ch: 14 sc and
13 ch-1 sps.

Repeat Rows 3 and 4 for
pattern until Cover measures
approximately 21" (53.5 cm) from
beginning ch, ending by working
Row 4.

Last Row: Ch 1, turn; sc in first
sc, ★ ch 1, skip next ch-1 sp, sc
in next sc; repeat from ★ across;
finish off.

Granny's Flower Blanket

■■□□ **EASY**

Finished Size: 43" (109 cm) square

SHOPPING LIST

Yarn (Super Bulky Weight)

Bernat® Baby Blanket™
[3.5 ounces, 86 yards
(100 grams, 78 meters) per skein]:
- ☐ Color A, #03005 White - 6 skeins
- ☐ Color B, #03200 Baby Pink -
  2 skeins
- ☐ Color C, #03615 Baby Yellow -
  1 skein

Crochet Hook
- ☐ Size M/N (9 mm) **or** size needed
  for gauge

GAUGE INFORMATION

In pattern,
   (3 dc, ch 1) twice = 4" (10 cm)
Gauge Swatch: 2³/₄" (7 cm)
   diameter
Work same as Blanket through
Rnd 1: 12 dc.

──── STITCH GUIDE ────

BEGINNING CLUSTER
   (uses one st)
Ch 2, ★ YO, insert hook in same
st, YO and pull up a loop, YO and
draw through 2 loops on hook;
repeat from ★ once **more**, YO and
draw through all 3 loops on hook.
CLUSTER (uses one dc)
★ YO, insert hook in dc indicated,
YO and pull up a loop, YO and
draw through 2 loops on hook;
repeat from ★ 2 times **more**, YO
and draw through all 4 loops on
hook.
DOUBLE CROCHET 3 TOGETHER
   (abbreviated dc3tog)
   (uses next 3 dc)
★ YO, insert hook in **next** dc, YO
and pull up a loop, YO and draw
through 2 loops on hook; repeat
from ★ 2 times **more**, YO and
draw through all 4 loops on hook.

INSTRUCTIONS

With Color C, ch 4; join with slip st
to form a ring.

Rnd 1 (Right side)**:** Ch 3 (**counts
as first dc, no and throughout**),
11 dc in ring; join with slip st to
first dc, finish off: 12 dc.

Note: Loop a short piece of yarn
around any stitch to mark Rnd 1
as **right** side.

Rnd 2: With **right** side facing, join
Color B with slip st in same st as
joining; work Beginning Cluster,
ch 3, work Cluster in next dc, ch 2,
skip next dc, ★ work Cluster in
next dc, ch 3, work Cluster in next
dc, ch 2, skip next dc; repeat from
★ 2 times **more**; join with slip st to
top of Beginning Cluster, finish off:
8 Clusters and 8 sps.

Rnd 3: With **right** side facing, join
Color A with dc in first ch-3 sp
(Fig. 4, page 47); 2 dc in same sp,
ch 1, 3 dc in next ch-2 sp, ch 1,
★ (3 dc, ch 3, 3 dc) in next ch-3 sp,
ch 1, 3 dc in next ch-2 sp, ch 1;
repeat from ★ 2 times **more**,
3 dc in same sp as first dc, ch 1,
sc in first dc to form last ch-3 sp:
12 3-dc groups and 12 sps.

Rnds 4-7: Ch 3, 2 dc in last ch-3 sp made, ch 1, (3 dc in next ch-1 sp, ch 1) across to next corner ch-3 sp, ★ (3 dc, ch 3, 3 dc) in corner ch-3 sp, ch 1, (3 dc in next ch-1 sp, ch 1) across to next corner ch-3 sp; repeat from ★ 2 times **more**, 3 dc in same corner sp as first dc, ch 1, sc in first dc to form last ch-3 sp: 28 3-dc groups and 28 sps.

Finish off.

Rnd 8: With **right** side facing, join Color B with dc in any corner ch-3 sp; 2 dc in same sp, ch 1, (3 dc in next ch-1 sp, ch 1) across to next corner ch-3 sp, ★ (3 dc, ch 3, 3 dc) in corner ch-3 sp, ch 1, (3 dc in next ch-1 sp, ch 1) across to next corner ch-3 sp; repeat from ★ 2 times **more**, 3 dc in same corner sp as first dc, ch 1, sc in first dc to form last ch-3 sp: 32 3-dc groups and 32 sps.

Rnd 9: Ch 3, 2 dc in last ch-3 sp made, ch 1, dc3tog, (ch 3, dc3tog) across to next corner ch-3 sp, ch 1, ★ (3 dc, ch 3, 3 dc) in corner ch-3 sp, ch 1, dc3tog, (ch 3, dc3tog) across to next corner ch-3 sp, ch 1; repeat from ★ 2 times **more**, 3 dc in same corner sp as first dc, ch 3; join with slip st to first dc, finish off: 40 sps.

Rnd 10: With **right** side facing, join Color A with dc in any corner ch-3 sp; 2 dc in same sp, ch 1, (3 dc in next sp, ch 1) across to next corner ch-3 sp, ★ (3 dc, ch 3, 3 dc) in corner ch-3 sp, ch 1, (3 dc in next sp, ch 1) across to next corner ch-3 sp; repeat from ★ 2 times **more**, 3 dc in same corner sp as first dc, ch 1, sc in first dc to form last ch-3 sp: 44 3-dc groups and 44 sps.

Rnds 11-13: Repeat Rnd 4, 3 times: 56 3-dc groups and 56 sps.

Finish off.

Rnds 14-19: Repeat Rnds 8-13: 84 3-dc groups and 84 sps.

Finish off.

Rnd 20: With **right** side facing, join Color C with slip st in first ch-1 sp after any corner; sc in next dc, 2 dc in next dc, sc in next dc, ★ (slip st in next ch-1 sp, sc in next dc, 2 dc in next dc, sc in next dc) across to next corner ch-3 sp, (sc, 2 dc, sc) in corner ch-3 sp, sc in next dc, 2 dc in next dc, sc in next dc; repeat from ★ around; join with slip st to first slip st, finish off.

Girl's Wave Blanket

 **EASY**

Finished Size: 35¹/₂" x 45" (90 cm x 114.5 cm)

SHOPPING LIST

Yarn (Super Bulky Weight)
Bernat® Baby Blanket™
[3.5 ounces, 86 yards
(100 grams, 78 meters) per skein]:
☐ Color A, #03200 Baby Pink -
4 skeins
☐ Color B, #03421 Little Petunias -
4 skeins

Crochet Hook
☐ Size N/P (10 mm) **or** size needed
for gauge

GAUGE INFORMATION

In pattern,
  2 repeats (24 sts) = 14¹/₂"
  (36.75 cm);
  4 rows = 5¹/₂" (14 cm)
Gauge Swatch: 14¹/₂"w x 5¹/₂"h
  (36.75 cm x 14 cm) from point to
  valley
With Color A, ch 24 **loosely**.
Row 1: Work same as Blanket:
23 dc.
Rows 2-4: Repeat Row 2 of
Blanket 3 times.
Finish off.

——STITCH GUIDE——

DOUBLE CROCHET 2 TOGETHER
  (abbreviated dc2tog)
  (uses next 2 sts)
★ YO, insert hook in **next** st, YO
and pull up a loop, YO and draw
through 2 loops on hook; repeat
from ★ once **more**, YO and draw
through all 3 loops on hook
(**counts as one dc**).

INSTRUCTIONS

With Color A, ch 60 **loosely**.

Row 1 (Right side)**:** Working in
back ridge of chs *(Fig. 1, page 47)*,
dc in third ch from hook, ★ † dc
in next 2 chs, 2 dc in next ch, dc
in next ch, 2 dc in next ch, dc in
next 2 chs, dc2tog †, dc in next ch,
dc2tog; repeat from ★ across to
last 9 chs, then repeat from † to †
once: 59 dc.

Note: Loop a short piece of yarn
around any stitch to mark Row 1
as **right** side.

Row 2: Ch 2, turn; skip first dc,
working in both loops, dc in next
3 dc, ★ † 2 dc in next dc, dc in next
dc, 2 dc in next dc, dc in next 2 dc,
dc2tog †, dc in next dc, dc2tog, dc
in next 2 dc; repeat from ★ across
to last 7 dc, then repeat from
† to † once.

Finish off.

Row 3: With **right** side facing and working in Back Loops Only *(Fig. 2, page 47)*, join Color B with slip st in first dc; ch 2, dc in next 3 dc, ★ † 2 dc in next dc, dc in next dc, 2 dc in next dc, dc in next 2 dc, dc2tog †, dc in next dc, dc2tog, dc in next 2 dc; repeat from ★ across to last 7 dc, then repeat from † to † once.

Rows 4-6: Repeat Row 2, 3 times.

Finish off.

Row 7: Using Color A, repeat Row 3.

Rows 8-10: Repeat Row 2, 3 times.

Finish off.

Rows 11-32: Repeat Rows 3-10 twice, then repeat Rows 3-8 once **more**.

Finish off.

Boy's Ripple Blanket

 **EASY**

Finished Size: 33" x 41½" (84 cm x 105.5 cm)

SHOPPING LIST

Yarn (Super Bulky Weight) **SUPER BULKY 6**
Bernat® Baby Blanket™
[3.5 ounces, 86 yards
(100 grams, 78 meters) per skein]:
☐ Color A, #03202 Baby Blue -
   4 skeins
☐ Color B, #03233 Funny Prints -
   4 skeins

Crochet Hook
☐ Size N/P (10 mm) **or** size needed
   for gauge

GAUGE INFORMATION

In pattern,
2 repeats (22 dc) = 13" (33 cm);
4 rows = 6½" (16.5 cm)

Gauge Swatch: 13"w x 6½"h
(33 cm x 16.5 cm) from
point to valley

With Color A, ch 26 **loosely.**

Row 1: Work same as Blanket:
23 dc and 2 ch-2 sps.

Rows 2-4: Repeat Row 2 of
Blanket 3 times.
Finish off.

——STITCH GUIDE——

DOUBLE CROCHET 2 TOGETHER
(abbreviated dc2tog)
(uses next 2 sts)
★ YO, insert hook in **next** st, YO
and pull up a loop, YO and draw
through 2 loops on hook; repeat
from ★ once **more**, YO and draw
through all 3 loops on hook
(counts as one dc).

DOUBLE CROCHET 3 TOGETHER
(abbreviated dc3tog)
(uses next 3 sts)
★ YO, insert hook in **next** st, YO
and pull up a loop, YO and draw
through 2 loops on hook; repeat
from ★ 2 times **more**, YO and
draw through all 4 loops on hook
(counts as one dc).

DECREASE (uses next 5 sts)
† YO, insert hook in **next** st, YO
and pull up a loop, YO and draw
through 2 loops on hook †; repeat
from † to † once, skip next st,
repeat from † to † twice, YO and
draw through all 5 loops on hook
(counts as one dc).

INSTRUCTIONS

With Color A, ch 62 **loosely**.

Row 1 (Right side)**:** Working in back ridge of chs *(Fig. 1, page 47)*, dc2tog beginning in third ch from hook, dc in next 3 chs, (2 dc, ch 2, 2 dc) in next ch, dc in next 3 chs, ★ decrease, dc in next 3 chs, (2 dc, ch 2, 2 dc) in next ch, dc in next 3 chs; repeat from ★ across to last 3 chs, dc3tog: 56 dc and 5 ch-2 sps.

Note: Loop a short piece of yarn around any stitch to mark Row 1 as **right** side.

Row 2: Ch 2, turn; skip first dc, dc2tog, dc in next 3 dc, (2 dc, ch 2, 2 dc) in next ch-2 sp, dc in next 3 dc, ★ decrease, dc in next 3 dc, (2 dc, ch 2, 2 dc) in next ch-2 sp, dc in next 3 dc; repeat from ★ across to last 3 dc, dc3tog.

Finish off.

Row 3: With **right** side facing, join Color B with slip st in first dc; ch 2, dc2tog, dc in next 3 dc, (2 dc, ch 2, 2 dc) in next ch-2 sp, dc in next 3 dc, ★ decrease, dc in next 3 dc, (2 dc, ch 2, 2 dc) in next ch-2 sp, dc in next 3 dc; repeat from ★ across to last 3 dc, dc3tog.

Rows 4-6: Repeat Row 2, 3 times.

Finish off.

Row 7: Using Color A, repeat Row 3.

Rows 8-10: Repeat Row 2, 3 times.

Finish off.

Rows 11-24: Repeat Rows 3-10 once, then repeat Rows 3-8 once **more**.

Finish off.

Play Mat

 **EASY**

Finished Size: 35¹/₂" (90 cm) square

SHOPPING LIST

Yarn (Super Bulky Weight)
Bernat® Baby Blanket™
[3.5 ounces, 86 yards
(100 grams, 78 meters) per skein]:
☐ #03010 Sand Baby - 8 skeins

Crochet Hook
☐ Size M/N (9 mm) **or** size needed
for gauge

GAUGE INFORMATION

In pattern,
   6 sts and 6 rows = 3¹/₂" (9 cm)
Gauge Swatch: 4" (10 cm) square
Ch 8 **loosely.**
Work same as Mat for 7 rows: 7 sts.
Finish off.

──STITCH GUIDE──

LONG SC

Working **around** previous row, insert hook in sc in row **below** next sc *(Fig. C),* YO and pull up a loop even with loop on hook, YO and draw through both loops on hook. Be sure that the Long sc is pulled up to the same height as the previous sc.

Fig. C

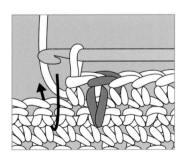

INSTRUCTIONS

Ch 62 **loosely.**

Row 1 (Right side)**:** Working in back ridge of chs *(Fig. 1, page 47),* sc in second ch from hook and in each ch across: 61 sc.

Row 2: Ch 1, turn; sc in each st across.

Row 3: Ch 1, turn; sc in first sc, (work Long sc, sc in next sc) across: 31 sc and 30 Long sc.

Row 4: Ch 1, turn; sc in each st across.

Row 5: Ch 1, turn; sc in first 2 sc, work Long sc, (sc in next sc, work Long sc) across to last 2 sc, sc in last 2 sc: 32 sc and 29 Long sc.

Repeat Rows 2-5 for pattern until Mat measures approximately 35" (89 cm) from beginning ch, ending by working Row 3 or Row 5.

Last Row: Ch 1, turn; sc in each st across; finish off.

General Instructions

ABBREVIATIONS

ch(s)	chain(s)
cm	centimeters
dc	double crochet(s)
dc2tog	double crochet 2 together
dc3tog	double crochet 3 together
hdc	half double crochet(s)
mm	millimeters
Rnd(s)	Round(s)
sc	single crochet(s)
sp(s)	space(s)
st(s)	stitch(es)
YO	yarn over

SYMBOLS & TERMS

★ — work instructions following ★ as many **more** times as indicated in addition to the first time.

( ) or **[ ]** — work enclosed instructions **as many** times as specified by the number immediately following **or** work all enclosed instructions in the stitch or space indicated **or** contains explanatory remarks.

† to † — work all instructions from first † to second † **as many** times as specified.

colon (:) — the number(s) given after a colon at the end of a row or round denote(s) the number of stitches or spaces you should have on that row or round.

GAUGE

Exact gauge is **essential** for proper size. Before beginning your project, make the sample swatch given in the individual instructions in the yarn and hook specified. After completing the swatch, measure it, counting your stitches and rows or rounds carefully. If your swatch is larger or smaller than specified, **make another, changing hook size to get the correct gauge**. Keep trying until you find the size hook that will give you the specified gauge.

CROCHET TERMINOLOGY

UNITED STATES		INTERNATIONAL
slip stitch (slip st)	=	single crochet (sc)
single crochet (sc)	=	double crochet (dc)
half double crochet (hdc)	=	half treble crochet (htr)
double crochet (dc)	=	treble crochet(tr)
treble crochet (tr)	=	double treble crochet (dtr)
double treble crochet (dtr)	=	triple treble crochet (ttr)
triple treble crochet (tr tr)	=	quadruple treble crochet (qtr)
skip	=	miss

Yarn Weight Symbol & Names	LACE (0)	SUPER FINE (1)	FINE (2)	LIGHT (3)	MEDIUM (4)	BULKY (5)	SUPER BULKY (6)
Type of Yarns in Category	Fingering, 10-count crochet thread	Sock, Fingering Baby	Sport, Baby	DK, Light Worsted	Worsted, Afghan, Aran	Chunky, Craft, Rug	Bulky, Roving
Crochet Gauge* Ranges in Single Crochet to 4" (10 cm)	32-42 double crochets**	21-32 sts	16-20 sts	12-17 sts	11-14 sts	8-11 sts	5-9 sts
Advised Hook Size Range	Steel*** 6,7,8 Regular hook B-1	B-1 to E-4	E-4 to 7	7 to I-9	I-9 to K-10.5	K-10.5 to M-13	M-13 and larger

*GUIDELINES ONLY: The chart above reflects the most commonly used gauges and hook sizes for specific yarn categories.

** Lace weight yarns are usually crocheted on larger-size hooks to create lacy openwork patterns. Accordingly, a gauge range is difficult to determine. Always follow the gauge stated in your pattern.

*** Steel crochet hooks are sized differently from regular hooks–the higher the number the smaller the hook, which is the reverse of regular hook sizing.

■□□□ BEGINNER	Projects for first-time crocheters using basic stitches. Minimal shaping.
■■□□ EASY	Projects using yarn with basic stitches, repetitive stitch patterns, simple color changes, and simple shaping and finishing.
■■■□ INTERMEDIATE	Projects using a variety of techniques, such as basic lace patterns or color patterns, mid-level shaping and finishing.
■■■■ EXPERIENCED	Projects with intricate stitch patterns, techniques and dimension, such as non-repeating patterns, multi-color techniques, fine threads, small hooks, detailed shaping and refined finishing.

CROCHET HOOKS															
U.S.	B-1	C-2	D-3	E-4	F-5	G-6	H-8	I-9	J-10	K-10½	L-11	M/N-13	N/P-15	P/Q	Q	S
Metric - mm	2.25	2.75	3.25	3.5	3.75	4	5	5.5	6	6.5	8	9	10	15	16	19

BACK RIDGE OF A CHAIN

Work only in loop(s) indicated by arrow *(Fig. 1)*.

Fig. 1

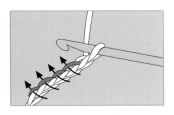

BACK & FRONT LOOPS ONLY

Work only in loop(s) indicated by arrow *(Fig. 2)*.

Fig. 2

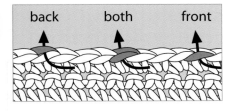

FREE LOOPS OF A CHAIN

When instructed to work in free loops of a chain, work in loop indicated by arrow *(Fig. 3)*.

Fig. 3

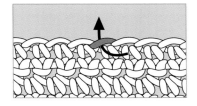

JOIN WITH DC

When instructed to join with dc, begin with a slip knot on hook. YO, holding loop on hook, insert hook in stitch or space indicated, YO and pull up a loop (3 loops on hook), (YO and draw through 2 loops on hook) twice *(Fig. 4)*.

Fig. 4

SLIP STITCH PIECES TOGETHER

To crochet pieces together to form a seam, hold pieces with **right** side together. Working through **both** loops of **both** layers *(Fig. 5a)*, or through **outer** loops of **both** layers *(Fig. 5b)*, slip st in each st across as specified in individual instructions.

Fig. 5a

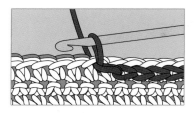

Fig. 5b

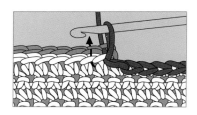

Instructions tested and photo models made by Janet Akins, Marianna Crowder, Lee Ellis, and Raymelle Greening.

Production Team: Writer/Technical Editor - Cathy Hardy; Editorial Writer - Susan Frantz Wiles; Senior Graphic Artist - Lora Puls; Graphic Artist - Jacqueline Breazeal; Photo Stylist - Sondra Daniel; and Photographer - Ken West.